As It Is

An Anthology of Intuitive Playfulness

By: Seb Rozo

Copyright © 2017 Seb Rozo

The Awakened Moment

All rights reserved.

ISBN-10: 0-692-95570-4
ISBN-13: 978-0-692-95570-3

Cover Design by Stephen Rozo

The space that is being looked for is the space that is looking.

- Rupert Spira -

CONTENT

Moments	-1-
Perception	-9-
Suffering	-23-
Expression	-33-
Insights	-41-
Emotion	-53-
Insights From A 10-Day Meditation Retreat	-61-
Creativity	-75-
Without Category	-87-
Reflections	-111-

DEDICATION

To: My family: Stephen, Ma, Pa, & Daisy.

To: The rest of my family, friends, mentors, strangers, and anyone who has supported and guided me in one way or another.

To: Fred Roden.

To: All living this Wonderful Mystery.

I wouldn't be the person I think I am without you.

May you prosper.

This is for you.

<3

DISCLAIMER

These are not ultimate truths. They should not be taken as medical, financial, or psychiatric advice. They are only symbols to point out other symbols of the Great Symbol.

At the end of the day, we are all guessing.

Moments

Truth can never be expressed through words.

Only through Silence.

Be completely <u>here</u> when walking, talking, breathing, playing, writing, typing, or doing anything.

Are you in your mind thinking, or are you actually doing the thing you're doing in this moment?

Do you actually feel the plastic keys touching your fingertips while typing?

Do you feel your body's weight resting on the chair?

Do you feel your crossed feet touching the cold tiled floor?

Do you feel your Breath's movement going in and out?

Are you in your body or are you in your head thinking while performing your actions?

This Life, this illusory sense of passing moments, is *always* pregnant with serendipitous opportunities we don't normally recognize.

These opportunities can be seen as part of our Grand Voyage consisting of: many smaller trips, memories, and emotions that all mingle and mesh into a single, unifying, confusing experience we call Life.

Enjoy every moment of this beautiful Life on Earth.

Enjoy every single moment, and recognize its ever-present Beauty.

We are alive! What more can we ask for?

Endless doors continuously present themselves for one to merge and flow into the Eternal Flow.

Most don't feel this Flow because they're so invested in the narrative the ego is feeding them through their thoughts.

To recognize and merge into this Flow, one must open the gates of the mind and throw their imaginary sense of self, I, ego over the precipice and into the abyss of the Unknown.

The pen pauses its dance waiting for words to flow through, endeavoring to reach as close to the significance of what is.

"What is" is just: is.

It's always there being Itself, waiting patiently for us to merge and surrender into its Isness.

Perception

When someone thinks a thought, their mind instantly forms an association and attachment that one usually doesn't catch in the moment.

The subtle crystallization of a thought goes like this:

You have a thought, it creates an association that your mind attaches to, and it stays in your memory. The more you recall this association through your memory, the more ingrained the thought becomes and the less possibility there is of new perspectives.

Over time these thoughts become more and more cemented and we eventually take these thoughts to be the foundation of who we think we are.

If these ingrained thoughts are ever threatened by others, we get offended because we have attached our sense of self to these thoughts and feel like we need to protect our self, or else we "die."

One must be attentive of when and where the mind teleports.

This mental teleportation, also referred to as: thinking, is usually triggered by our mind's projections and fears about the future and its imagined past.

The mind is continuously rewriting the story of who it thinks it is through our thoughts and we continuously believe the narrative being spewed forth.

It does this all in a very, very cute attempt to make sense of this whole Mystery we live in.

We must continuously catch ourselves when teleporting to "distant" regions, knowing that we aren't really going anywhere.

The only place we're ever really in is:

Here.

What is meditation?

Meditation is anything that quiets the mind and merges you into the Eternal Symphony of Everythingness.

Where there are no opposites.

Where one is a no-one and no-one is one.

The mind will keep trying to reel you back in, attempting to tell you who you think you are.

But guess what?

You are not that…

whatever the ego is promising you.

A seeker of Truth is always hungry to contemplate new ways of looking at familiar things.

No one Thing is better than another.

All Things are entry-points into the Divine.

Labeling thoughts as "good "or "bad" is a fool's errand.

Observing them is enough until the next step is revealed.

One must be the scientist of one's own Soul.

Observe. Apply. Experience.

Observations of "others" are observations of your own self.

Altering your perception is your own responsibility, enjoyment, & experience.

Not the government's nor your parent's.

All mental states are ultimately transient.

Think of them as signposts, guides, and bridges to the Doors of Infinity.

Moments cannot be grasped.

Only enjoyed.

☺

Suffering

Our anxieties originate from the same place: the mind. The mind starts thinking of something it has to do in the future while its already in the middle of something in the present, so one starts compromising the awareness of the present activity by:

1st: rushing through whatever one is currently doing to do the other imagined future thing which

2nd: leads to further anxiety that you have to complete something after that future thing, in an endless rushed cycle.

This is how most of us are living in varying degrees.

Attach to the least amount of things possible.

First, start mentally and the rest follows.

Many Things give us pleasure and feelings of euphoria, such as: people, music, movies, food, drugs, vacations, objects, and activities. But ultimately, they are ephemeral, limited, and impermanent.

The more we indulge in them, the more we grow tired with them and they lose their initial appeal.

Instead of seeing these Things as ends in themselves, we must use them as instruments to experience and enjoy the Continuous Energy that is graciously being poured into us at all times.

Be free from all self-imposed limitations and fears.

How does one be free from them?

Recognize limitations and doubts as nothing more than negative thoughts you thought of one day, convinced yourself that they were true, and then forgot this very process ever happened.

Everyone is currently going through their own uniquely crafted journey, pegged with their own obstacles in the way of their desires.

One of our missions in this Life, I believe, is to go through our own obstacles while simultaneously relieving each other's suffering.

Everyone's got their own antagonists.

We must support each other in transcending them.

Judging is a necessary prerequisite to fully understand Compassion.

In a relative sense, we naturally gravitate towards anything that we believe will take us closer to our projected vision of peace, happiness, and security.

In the ultimate sense, we naturally gravitate towards anything we believe will take us closer to Where We Came From/ Our Creator/ Our Self.

Expression

Find the Beauty in others and let it be known to them.

We should always aspire to the best of our perceived potential, always knowing that there exists a greater potential behind that one.

No one's truly boring.

A boring person just doesn't know how to effectively express their internal world yet.

There's a theme and purpose to every single conversation.

And Attention is one of the Highest forms of currency there is.

No one can just hand Truth to someone else, neither through language or writing.

The most we can do is guide, support, and evoke the Truth out of an "other."

The intent that you do anything with will be felt and understood by others at the subtlest levels.

Whenever speaking, moving, or doing anything, ask yourself:

Where is the intention coming from?

What are the motives or agendas behind this?

Who is it that is asking these questions?

If you locate the questioner, you solve the riddle…

Partially.

Insights

Our lens of Life, our perceptual framework in how we view this Mystery, is shaped by our thoughts, memories, experiences, and range of insights over our Lifetime…

Most importantly: how we've applied each one.

Each level of philosophy is necessary for each person… wherever they might be.

Each level is part of the All, which leads to the same Place.

Insights tend to follow a hierarchical dynamic:

A previous insight will usually transform itself into a much Higher quality insight, which then leads to another Higher quality one, and another one, and another one…all moving in a beautifully linked mandala, with each insight being revealed in its most perfectly imperfect moment.

As time passes in one's Life, one sees certain ideas and creative insights reveal themselves in a given moment.

These ideas and insights, that flash in one's Consciousness, serve the purpose of possibly being explored at that moment.

It is upto one's will, interest, and intuitive pull to see if it's personally worth to explore the idea further.

If one ends up pursuing the path of an insight, it inevitably unleashes an array of doors waiting to be opened. And one begins a journey for however long it takes.

The biggest mistake is envisioning complete fulfillment once one "arrives" at that imaginary end place.

The journey is an end in itself.

Every single moment of it.

There's nowhere to get to, or arrive.

It's all Here-Now.

Enjoy.

Pursue the creative insights that makes one feel alive, light, and joyful.

This Feeling expresses Itself as a subtle quality of freedom and fluttering other-worldliness coming from the Heart center and radiating through the body.

We've all experienced this Feeling before but can never quite describe what it is.

Over time and experience, one recognizes, and is guided by, this Feeling much easier.

Whatever you choose to see, you see.

One intuitive realization is worth more than twenty thousand rational thoughts.

Our thoughts and insights are the lenses we use to view our Life, which attach themselves to our body: the camera.

Ultimately, lenses are transitory…and so is the camera.

Emotion

Anger presents itself when something doesn't go the way we wanted it to go.

We must ask ourselves, and figure out, why we wanted it a certain way.

What is embarrassment?

The moment wherein any action, speech, or situation happens where your ego feels threatened of its built up identity.

Its reputation is compromised and a strange kind of fear sets in one's body and mind.

The ego feels like its death is impending, thus losing everything it has worked so hard in the past to uphold and maintain.

Fear is a doorway to Transformation.

Deep within, we have an infinite storehouse of Love that is screaming for access and expression.

Most of us have forgotten that it's even there…

This lack of access and expression manifests as frustration, anger, and depression because we feel we have lost the map to get back Home.

There can never be a logical explanation for Love.

Insights from a 10-Day Meditation Retreat

8 days of no talking, eye contact, or communication with another human being.

10-hour days of spread out Vipassana meditation, Silence, and doing nothing but being with one's own mind and body.

Listen and feel predominantly from the Heart center, not from the head center.

This thought shall pass...

and this one...

and this one too...

Infinite analogies present themselves to us from the Infinite Analogy.

Rocks are friends.

Nature continuously teaches.

Accept every moment and corresponding thoughts with full acceptance and equanimity.

Return to the Breath, when needed.

Every moment is grist for the mill.

Everything is dancing in different rhythms to the same Eternal Song.

Impermanence.

Everything is in constant flux.

Everything.

We are consistently reacting to each thought that comes across our mental landscape, and most times not even knowing that we are reacting.

Are thoughts coming from a balanced place (as it is) or from a manipulative place (how you want it to be)?

We are constantly identifying with thoughts and feelings. As soon as you feel a craving or aversion to a thought or feeling, that is an immediate red flag.

Try to watch each reaction you have to each thought.

Accept them, feel their intensity, and let them pass.

You are not them.

You are much More.

All sensations, thoughts, and things labelled as "good," or "bad," are illusory.

Look at them as they are and know that they will pass.

We aren't addicted to certain people, experiences, or things…we are addicted to the sensations they give us.

In meditation and waking life, place your attention on feeling your whole body inside and out, moment after moment.

Prolong these intervals of returning and Being your body.

If your attention is on the body, the mind cannot distract you as easily.

There are 3 ways your thoughts can go:

1. Craving: Comes from desire and attachment.

2. Aversion: Also comes from desire and attachment.

(These 2 come from and lead to further ignorance)

3. Being: Observing and letting each thought flow and go without believing and continuing the imagined narrative.

What I missed and desired:

- Communication
- Physical touch
- Eye contact
- Kissing/Sex
- Ordinary chit-chat
- Being creative and creating things
- Exercising
- Randomness and Mystery of <u>ordinary</u> Life and its events
- Serving and helping others
- Writing
- Home

Things I resisted:

- Authority (being told what to do).
- Being forced to do something.
- Sticking through a routine.
- Feelings of boredom (misery).

Creativity

Art: the representation of opposites harmonizing.

What an artist does for a spectator is express an insight, thought, or idea that both connect with in a subtle and familiar way.

There are infinite entry-points into the Divine, with a plethora of mediums to do so.

You discern which mediums are most resonant and enjoyable for you to share your self with others.

Metaphors and analogies are the Highest instruments in bridging every level of understanding.

We do not arrive somewhere randomly.

Tune into your environment, your self, and others to see what's possible to find out and create.

Every story we tell is the story we need in that exact moment.

We use other people's quotes because either:

a) We agree with their insight.

b) They have articulated an insight we have had before and enjoy how they worded it.

c) We want to continue the quote's momentum for posterity purposes.

and/or

d) Pushing your own quote would be awkward and disgraceful.

Simplicity in complexity is the Highest form of sophistication.

Your Muse is always Here…waiting to create the next masterpiece through you.

Create, others will interpret.

Without Category

Whatever you wish you knew much earlier is a complete waste of time and energy.

It's Here-Now and runs on its own schedule.

Perfection is unknowable, yet within us at all times.

Others give us meaning in Life.

Intention is everything.

Balance is everything.

Create more opportunities for others to tell the truth.

Everyone, at whichever stage of Life they're at, craves communion with That which we all came from.

If one takes the view that Life is ultimately a perfect arrangement and harmony, then why does one believe in doubt, worry, and anxiety?

Every single Thing around us, on top, within, bottom, sideways, and diagonal in the Kosmos is completely in our favor. It is All for us: every single cell, neutron, proton, molecule, quantum, and sub-atomic particle divided by 64 and square rooted, is all for us.

We need only recognize it.

Life is like

Religion is not a fixed entity. It is only a framework we collectively create and agree upon, according to the personality of a particular time period, to attempt to make sense of this Whole Mystery.

Writing things down is both crucial and useless.

We read books in order to find the perfectly ordered words that will liberate us out of our current prison of understanding.

Books are instruments to help illuminate any spaces of our minds we have failed to see ourselves.

Read something because it pulls you in a super subtle and attractive-magnetic kind of way.

If it doesn't, drop it.

It is way too easy to forget that the reason we possess things is to be able to share them with others.

We are all a bunch of walking mirrors,

reflecting each other's Perfection.

The Play plays its Play.

All alls in the All.

Space spaces in Space.

When someone gives you advice, they mean to give it to themselves

…and vice versa.

Understand thy mother & father.

Thank thy mother & father.

Strive to always be the last one to pull away from a hug.

The Breath & Death are the sureties of one's Life.

The appearance of one signifies the temporary absence of the other.

Silence follows Silence.

No one person has all the answers,

nor ever will.

Reflections

All questions are arbitrary so why not ask the most arbitrary ones?

Do I know things because I actually know them?

or

Do I know things because I pretend to know them?

What is memory but the memory of memory…

Can variables be as constant as constants?

What if thinking logically/rationally is just practice for thinking intuitively?

Why do I continuously lie to myself and others?

What would I like to do before I inevitably die?

How terrible would it be if this whole Mystery of Life could be defined through words?

Life: As It Is.

ABOUT THE AUTHOR

Seb Rozo is a guy who listened to what was being spoken through him and crafted those sound bites into cute one-liners and such.

He thanks and honors you for spending your precious time in absorbing and reflecting on these things.

You can reach him at:

sebastianrozo5@gmail.com

or

www.sebrozo.com

All is One.

enjoy

COVER DESIGNED BY
STEPHEN ROZO

ISBN 9780692955703